I0844956

Introduction

Colors are a world of magic and beauty, and a dazzling elegance that gives things beauty and splendor. Colors are the beautiful secret that God Almighty deposited in everything he created in the vast universe. Nature abounds in the delightful colors that give things their meaning, and in every color a secret is what is hidden in it , And many tales filled with books and notebooks and stored by myths and mothers' tales, and this is why God Almighty, when He gave everything in nature a color, made these colors in the highest harmony, to be comfortable to look, beautiful and charming, the blue for the sky and the sea, green for the trees, yellow for the sun, and bright colors Beautiful flowers and Birds, and many other great colors that increase the level of beauty.

THIS COLOR IS

Paste the appropriate color

THIS COLOR IS

GREEN

Paste the appropriate color

THIS COLOR IS

YELLOW

Paste the appropriate color

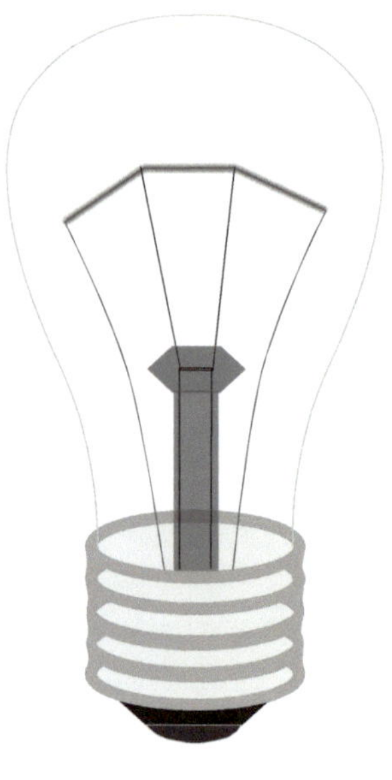

THIS COLOR IS

PINK

Paste the appropriate color

THIS COLOR IS

ORANGE

Paste the
appropriate
color

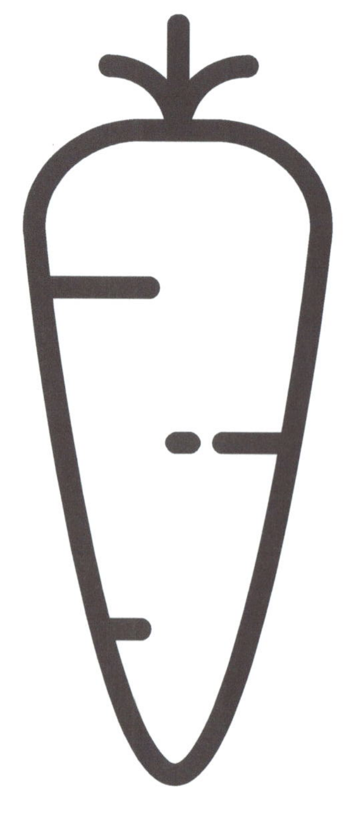

THIS COLOR IS

BLUE

Paste the appropriate color

THIS COLOR IS BLACK

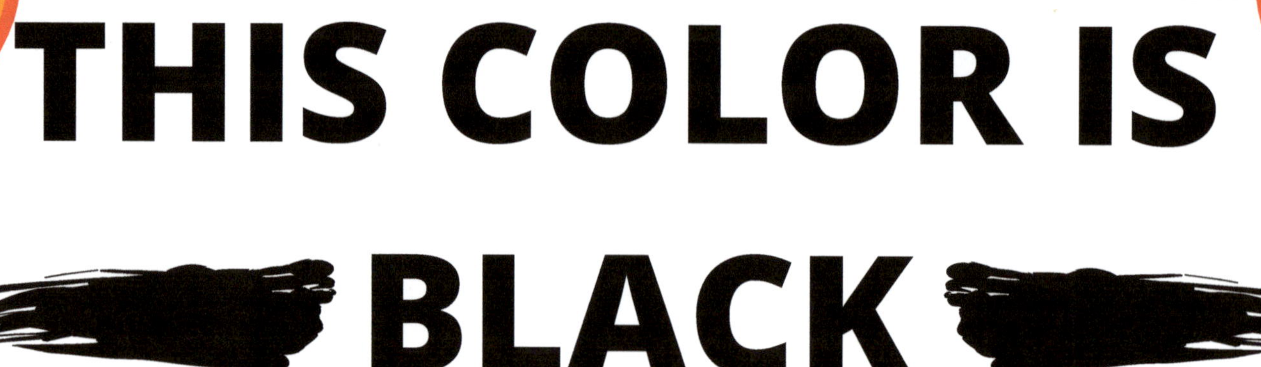

Paste the appropriate color

THIS COLOR IS

GRAY

THIS COLOR IS

THIS COLOR IS

CYAN

THIS COLOR IS

PURPLE

Paste the
appropriate
color

THIS COLOR IS

BROWN

Paste the appropriate color

White is the color that reflects black, and it is one of the neutral colors that fit almost all other colors, and white is often associated with goodness, purity, and serenity, which is why girls wear them on their wedding day, so angels are often depicted in white, as the color was linked White to provide health care, it is the color worn by doctors and nurses, as white is one of the colors that go into designing clothes, whether in summer or winter, and white color is also commonly used in simple designs.